Scripture and the Wesleyan Way
Leader Guide

Scripture and the Wesleyan Way
A Bible Study on Real Christianity

Book

978-1-5018-6793-4

978-1-5018-6794-1 eBook

DVD

978-1-5018-6797-2

Leader Guide

978-1-5018-6795-8

978-1-5018-6796-5 eBook

For more information, visit AbingdonPress.com.

Also by Scott J. Jones and Arthur D. Jones

Ask: Faith Questions in a Skeptical Age

Also by Scott J. Jones

The Wesleyan Way: A Faith That Matters

The Once and Future Wesleyan Movement

The Future of The United Methodist Church:
Seven Vision Pathways (Ed. with Bruce Ough)

Staying at the Table: The Gift of Unity for United Methodists

The Evangelistic Love of God and Neighbor:
A Theology of Witness and Discipleship

United Methodist Doctrine: The Extreme Center

John Wesley's Conception and Use of Scripture

Scripture

AND THE

Wesleyan Way

A Bible Study on Real Christianity

LEADER GUIDE

SCOTT J. JONES AND ARTHUR D. JONES

Alex Joyner
Abingdon Press / Nashville

Scripture and the Wesleyan Way
A Bible Study on Real Christianity
Leader Guide

978-1-5018-6795-8

18 19 20 21 22 23 24 25 26 27 — 10 9 8 7 6 5 4 3 2 1
MANUFACTURED IN THE UNITED STATES OF AMERICA

Contents

To the Group Leader 7

Chapter 1. What Is the Bible's Message? 15

Chapter 2. How Can I Be Saved? 23

Chapter 3. Am I a Real Christian? 31

Chapter 4. Do I Have to Obey the Law? 39

Chapter 5. Am I a Sinner? 47

Chapter 6. How Can I Connect with God? 55

Chapter 7. Why Is the Christian Life So Hard? 63

Chapter 8. What About My Money? .71

Sermons of John Wesley 79

To the Group Leader

Overview of the Study

Scripture and the Wesleyan Way: A Bible Study on Real Christianity by Scott and Arthur Jones is an invitation to a richer experience of the Christian life. Bishop Scott Jones and the Rev. Arthur Jones are dedicated United Methodist leaders who share John Wesley's conviction that by taking the early church and the Bible seriously we can discover a message that is as relevant today as it was in Wesley's era. John Wesley's method of reading Scripture highlights God's transforming love for individuals. The authors believe it can also renew the church.

The method of study used in this book begins with basic spiritual questions that many people have. Each of the eight chapters looks at a different question and then looks at the biblical witness with this question in mind. Concluding sections in each chapter show how Wesley applied the Bible to answer the question and to illuminate something that was of great concern to Wesley—the story of God's salvation. The hymns of John's brother, Charles Wesley, contributed to this story as well, so each chapter concludes with the text of a hymn, usually by Charles.

In this book and through this study, you will encounter the Bible and the Wesleyan witness in new and powerful ways. But the goal of this study is not to have a lot of "head knowledge" of Scripture. The authors claim that John Wesley, like Jesus, had a practical nature and he saw "searching the Scriptures" as a path to transformed lives. As you and your group participate in this study, if you find yourselves growing in your love of God and your neighbor, then you will have experienced the power of the Wesleyan Way.

Session Themes

Below are the chapter titles, which are also the key questions for each session, along with a description of the main idea in each chapter. These summaries are used, beginning with session 4, as part of the session plans to review "The Wesleyan Way of Salvation."

1. What Is the Bible's Message?

The Bible's central message is the kingdom of God, which is marked by righteousness, peace, and joy. We experience it through repentance and faith.

2. How Can I Be Saved?

Salvation is a present and future reality. We experience it through justification, which changes our relationship with God, and sanctification, which is a process of transformation in us. Salvation comes through faith alone but results in good works.

3. Am I a Real Christian?

Sanctification includes the expectation that we can experience salvation now through loving God and loving others, as expressed in Jesus' Great Commandment.

4. Do I Have to Obey the Law?

We are saved by grace through faith, but sanctification is a lifelong journey and the moral law has a role as it draws us toward perfection.

5. Am I a Sinner?

We all are impacted by the power of sin and are unable to save ourselves. Jesus the Great Physician forgives and heals that sin.

6. How Can I Connect with God?

God provides us with the means of grace to help us maintain and grow in our connection to God. Among these are prayer, Bible reading, Holy Communion, fasting, and Christian conferencing.

7. Why Is the Christian Life So Hard?

Repentance is not only a turning back to God but a complete transformation of our hearts. Believers can experience real, inward change but only through ongoing repentance.

8. What About My Money?

Money, like grace, is a gift from God. When we structure our lives to reflect our faith, including giving money to God, we open ourselves to continuing transformation.

Session Plans

This leader's guide will help you lead an eight-session study of *Scripture and the Wesleyan Way: A Bible Study on Real Christianity* with a group of learners. The sections of each session are clearly laid out, and they are based on the structure of the book. You will find the lesson plans easy to use, with sufficient material for every session. In fact, you may have more than you need, so you can choose from the options in each section to tailor the study to your group and allotted time.

The study includes eight sessions based on the eight chapters of the book. It makes use of the following components:

- the book *Scripture and the Wesleyan Way: A Bible Study on Real Christianity*, by Scott and Arthur Jones;
- the DVD that accompanies the study; and
- this Leader Guide.

Participants in the study should plan on bringing Bibles and the *Scripture and the Wesleyan Way* book to each session. If possible, notify those interested in the study in advance of the first session. Make arrangements for them to get copies of the book so that they can read the introduction and chapter 1 prior to the first group meeting.

Using This Guide with Your Group

This guide has been designed to give you flexibility and choice in tailoring the sessions for your group. The session format is listed below. You may choose any or all of the activities, adapting them as you wish to meet the schedule and needs of your particular group.

This Leader Guide offers a basic session plan with material sufficient for 90-minute sessions, but if your group is meeting for 60 minutes or a shorter period, select fewer options while maintaining at least one element from each section. Select ahead of time which activities the group will do, for how long, and in what order. Depending on which activities you select, special preparation may be required. The "Before Class" section describes what advance preparation is needed for each session.

Session Format

- *Session Summary:* A brief description of the content and themes of the chapter on which the session is based.
- *Before Class:* Describes any preparation that is required before the group meets.
- *Welcome:* Opening activities that introduce the theme of the session, including an opening prayer.
- *Bible Study and Discussion:* Options for exercises that explore the key Scripture passages for this chapter.
- *Video Study and Discussion:* Exercises to help the group discuss the video for the session, including a brief summary of the video content.
- *Book Study and Discussion:* Activities and options for discussing the book chapter, including insights from Wesley's sermons and exercises to connect the content with everyday life.
- *Close the Session:* Closing activities to review learnings and consider commitments to follow up. Includes suggestions related to a group reading or singing of the hymn that concludes the chapter.

Helpful Hints

Preparing for the Session

- Begin your preparation in prayer. Pray that participants will be able to experience a richer Christian life through this study. Pray for the leading of the Holy Spirit as you prepare for the study.
- Before each session, familiarize yourself with the content. Read the book chapter again, making notes as you go.
- Depending on the length of time you have available for group meetings, you may or may not have time to do all the activities. Select the activities in advance that will work for your group time and interests.
- Choose the session elements you will use during the group session, including the specific discussion questions you plan to cover. Be prepared, however, to adjust the session as group members interact and as questions arise. Prepare carefully, but allow space for the Holy Spirit to move in and through the group members and through you as the facilitator.

- Prepare the room where the group will meet so that the space will enhance the learning process. Ideally, group members should be seated around a table or in a circle so that all can see each other. Special seating arrangements for some sessions are also suggested in the planning notes.
- Bring a supply of Bibles for those who forget to bring their own.
- For most sessions you will also need a whiteboard and markers or an easel with large sheets of paper and markers.

Shaping the Learning Environment

- Begin and end on time.
- Create a climate of openness, encouraging group members to participate as they feel comfortable.
- Remember that some people will jump right in with answers and comments, while others need time to process what is being discussed.
- If you notice that some group members are not entering the conversation, ask them if they have thoughts to share. Give everyone a chance to talk, but keep the conversation moving. Moderate to prevent a few individuals from doing all the talking.
- If no one answers at first during discussions, do not be afraid of silence. Count silently to ten, then say something such as, "Would anyone like to go first?" If no one responds, venture an answer yourself and ask for comments.
- Model openness as you share with the group. Group members will follow your example. If you limit your sharing to a surface level, others will follow suit.
- Encourage multiple answers or responses before moving on.
- To help continue a discussion and give it greater depth, ask, "Why?" or "Why do you believe that?" or "Can you say more about that?"
- Affirm others' responses with comments such as "Great" or "Thanks" or "Good insight," especially if it's the first time someone has spoken during the group session.
- Monitor your own contributions. If you are doing most of the talking, back off so that you do not train the group to listen rather than speak up.

- Remember that your role is not to have all the answers. Your job is to keep the discussion going and encourage participation.

Managing the Session

- Honor the time schedule. If a session is running longer than expected, get consensus from the group before continuing beyond the agreed-upon ending time.
- Involve group members in various aspects of the group session, such as saying prayers or reading the Scripture.
- Note that the session plans sometimes call for breaking into smaller groups. This gives everyone a chance to speak and participate fully. Mix up the groups; don't let the same people pair up for every activity.
- As always in discussions that may involve personal sharing, confidentiality is essential. Group members should never pass along stories that have been shared in the group. Remind the group members at each session: confidentiality is crucial to the success of this study.

Optional Activities

To enrich your group's experience, consider using one of the following optional activities in addition to each week's lesson plan.

1) *Reading Wesley's Sermons—Scripture and the Wesleyan Way* refers to and summarizes one of John Wesley's sermons in each chapter. Wesley's eighteenth-century language can be difficult, but you can offer group members a deeper experience of Wesley by inviting volunteers to read the sermons ahead of time and share their insights with the group. Beginning with the closing exercises of Session 1, the session plan includes the option of assigning a sermon for the upcoming week to a participant. Tell the volunteer that you will be asking him or her to share insights and impressions of the sermon at the next session. Don't require persons to participate in this activity.

The sermons used in this study can be found in *John Wesley's Sermons: An Anthology*, eds. Albert C. Outler and Richard P. Heitzenrater (Nashville: Abingdon Press, 1991). The 1872 edition of the sermons, edited by Thomas Jackson, can be found at the Wesley Center Online, which can be accessed at http://wesley.nnu.edu/?id=787.

2) *Journaling*—Another way to encourage deeper engagement with the material outside of the group sessions is to recommend that participants get a journal to use throughout the study. The journal can be as simple as a composition notebook. Encourage group members to write questions and insights in the journal as they read through the study book each week. They may also use it for some of the exercises in class that require individual work.

Session 1

What Is the Bible's Message?

Session Summary

In the introduction to *Scripture and the Wesleyan Way*, the authors express their conviction that John Wesley's approach to Scripture can help us read the Bible faithfully and renew the church. In each of the chapters of this book, the authors present a spiritual question and explore its importance for us today. They look at biblical texts related to these questions and at a sermon by John Wesley in which he did the same thing.

Chapter 1 focuses on the question "What is the Bible's message?" Scott and Arthur Jones present two truths about the Bible—that it is important and that it is complicated—and explore four Wesleyan principles for acknowledging these truths and discerning the Bible's message. The authors propose that one of the most important messages in the Bible is about the kingdom of God. Wesley's sermon "The Way to the Kingdom" provides us with a vision of what that kingdom is and isn't and affirms the ways the individual believer can experience a true "religion of the heart" through trusting God's life-changing love revealed in Jesus Christ. Charles Wesley's famous hymn "Love Divine, All Loves Excelling" describes how that love can change our hearts.

Before Class

- On a large sheet of paper, write the following incomplete sentence: "The Bible's primary message is..." Place the sheet in a prominent location in the meeting area that is accessible to participants. Alternatively, write these words on a portion of a whiteboard.
- On another large sheet of paper (or another section of the whiteboard) write the words of Romans 14:17 in the translation used in the book (KJV): "The kingdom of God is not meat and drink; but righteousness, and peace, and joy in the Holy Ghost."
- Post another large sheet of paper (or reserve a third section of whiteboard) for the exercise titled "Understanding the Religion of the Heart."
- Have Bibles available for group members who may not bring their own.
- Provide markers of varied colors, pencils, pens, and blank paper for use during the session.
- Since this is the first session, have name tags available if the participants do not know one another.

Welcome

As persons enter, ask them to make a name tag and put it on. Then, invite them to choose a marker and complete the incomplete sentence on the sheet you placed on the wall before the class began ("The Bible's primary message is..."), writing their responses below the heading.

Once everyone has arrived, introduce yourself to the group and say that you are going to begin with an exercise to help persons get to know each other a little better. Ask each participant to find a partner, preferably someone they don't know very well. Once they are together, ask them to share their names with each other and then choose which of the pair will go first in the following exercise.

Explain that you are going to ask them to talk about a topic for sixty seconds (you will need to time them). During those sixty seconds, the first person will speak and the other person will listen silently. Then, at your cue, they will switch roles and the second person will talk for sixty seconds on the same subject. When everyone is ready, give the following prompt:

- For sixty seconds, talk about a book, TV show, or movie and why you liked it.

After both persons have shared, have them do the exercise again with a new prompt:

- For sixty seconds, tell a story about a favorite Bible in your house.

Now have each person introduce their partner to the whole group, sharing one thing they learned from listening to them.

Read the following introduction to this first session of the study, or use one of your own:

- Welcome to this study of the book *Scripture and the Wesleyan Way* by Scott Jones and Arthur Jones. Each time we gather, we are going to be looking at an important spiritual question that you may have wondered about at some point during your life. Using the Bible, the book, and the video segments, we are going to look at those questions and how John Wesley, one of the founders of the Methodist movement, answered them. Our hope is that we will grow closer to God and to one another through this study. Our question for this session is "What Is the Bible's Message?"

Review —See Notes

Bible Study and Discussion

[This Bible Study may be used at this point or following the exercise titled "Share Experiences with the Bible" in the Book Study and Discussion section.]

One of the key ways that Jesus talks about the kingdom of God in the Gospels is through the use of parables. In the following exercise you will have a chance to look at some of those parables and what they tell us about the nature of the Kingdom.

Divide into four groups, giving each group one of the following Scripture passages to read:

- Matthew 13:31-33: the parables of the mustard seed and yeast
- Mark 4:26-29: the parable of the seed growing in the ground
- Matthew 13:44-46: the parables of the treasure in the field and the pearl
- Matthew 13:1-9, 18-23: the parable of the sower

Ask each group to use the following questions to explore their assigned passage:

- To what is the kingdom of God being compared?
- How might this image upset our expectations of what a kingdom is?

- What do you believe Jesus is trying to say about the nature of God's kingdom?

After some time of discussion in the small group, gather with the larger group to share observations.

Now read together Romans 14:17 from the paper you prepared and posted on the wall before the group arrived. Say to the group:

- The authors of this study make the point that the kingdom of God is a central message of Jesus' ministry and of the Bible. This verse from Romans is one of the main Bible texts of John Wesley's sermon "The Way to the Kingdom."

Ask the group to reflect on the following questions together:

- What does Romans 14:17 tell us that the kingdom of God is not? What does that mean?
- What does it say that the kingdom of God is?
- How do righteousness, peace, and joy in the Holy Spirit help us understand Jesus' images of the Kingdom in the parables?

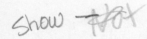 *Show*

Video Study and Discussion

Play the video for Session 1.

After viewing the video segment, choose some of the following questions to explore with the group:

- The video talks about how Scott Jones helped Arthur learn the fruit of the Spirit from Galatians 5. If you have memorized a part of the Bible, what is it? How did you learn it?
- What does it mean to read, as Wesley did, for the "general tenor" of Scripture?
- What is the Wesleyan way of reading Scripture?
- How can the same Scripture speak to us differently in different seasons of our lives?
- Where do the authors suggest starting to read the Bible? Why?

Gospels

Book Study and Discussion

Discuss the Wesleys

Say the following to the group:

- In the introduction to the book, the authors point out that people in the Wesleyan tradition look to John and Charles Wesley, not as perfect models, but as reliable guides to a faithful way of taking the Scriptures seriously and renewing the church. In the first chapter, the authors say that John Wesley's main concern in interpreting the Bible is "how a person can be saved from sin and for salvation."

Discuss with the group the following questions:

- Why are the concerns of the Wesleys still relevant to us today?
- What is salvation as you understand it?
- How does sin injure our relationship with God?

Share Experiences with the Bible

Invite three volunteers to share briefly a time when reading the Bible was important to them.

- What made it meaningful?

Now ask the group:

- Why do Christians feel that the Bible is important?

Invite three more volunteers to share briefly a time when the Bible has seemed difficult to them.

- What made it so?

Ask the group:

- What frustrations do we have in understanding the Bible?

Share that the focus of the first chapter is on the following spiritual question: "The Bible is both important and complicated. So what is its message?"

Turn to the sheet posted on the wall on which you asked participants to complete the incomplete sentence ["The Bible's primary message is . . ."]. Read the responses that are written and invite participants to clarify where they wish. Ask:

- What do you observe about the responses we gave?
- What do they have in common, and how do they differ from one another?
- What do they say about what we believe about the Bible?
- How would John Wesley complete this sentence?

Read the first two sentences of the section of the chapter titled "Wesley's Answer" on page 18 to remind group members of Wesley's emphasis on the kingdom of God. [*You may want to move into the Bible Study following this exercise if you did not do it earlier.*]

Explore the Four Wesleyan Principles

Say:

- The authors of this book outline four principles that John Wesley used in determining the message of the Bible. We're going to explore them in this next exercise.

Divide into four groups. Assign each group one of the four principles found near the beginning of chapter 1 in the study book (see pages 11–15). Ask them to read the section related to their assigned principle and prepare to present it to the whole group. To organize the presentation, the small groups should assume that they are speaking to people who have not read the book.

After some time for reading and preparation, have each group present to the total group briefly.

As a total group, discuss the following questions:

- What is helpful about this way of reading the Bible?
- Which of these principles seems challenging to you?

Understanding the Religion of the Heart

Say:

- As the authors point out, John Wesley felt that Christianity is "a religion of the heart," and that human beings need to have a transformative experience of God. In the section on Wesley's answer to the question of what the Bible's message is, the authors explain how Wesley understood "righteousness, peace, and joy in the Holy Spirit"—the three characteristics of the kingdom of God in Romans 14:17.

P. 18

For each of the three characteristics—righteousness, peace, and joy—ask group members to find definitions from their reading of the study book in the section "Wesley's Answer." Write the definitions on a large piece of paper posted on the wall.

After completing this exercise, ask:

- How do these definitions differ from what you would expect?
- How do we still long for these today?

Close the Session

Invite Someone to Read a Wesley Sermon (optional)

The leader helps at the beginning of this Leader Guide include a note under "Optional Activities" about where Wesley's sermons can be found (page 12). As a way of giving participants an immersion experience in Wesley, ask for a volunteer each session to read the sermon for the following session and bring back a brief report on it. Tell them that you will be asking them to share their impressions of Wesley's central point and highlights of the sermon that they noted. Advise the volunteers that Wesley's eighteenth-century language may be a little difficult. The sermon for the next session is "The Scripture Way of Salvation."

Do a Self-Inventory

Say:

- John Wesley's sermon on the "The Way to the Kingdom" begins with Jesus' message in Mark 1:15. Wesley points out two key commandments in this verse: repent and believe. When we do an honest inventory of ourselves, we discover that there are many places where we desire to turn around and seek God's forgiveness.

Distribute pieces of paper to participants and ask them to begin a self-inventory of areas in their lives where they would like to turn around and seek forgiveness. Assure them that they will not have to share this inventory with anyone and that they can take the paper with them and continue the exercise in their prayer time during the week.

Allow a few minutes for this exercise, with participants working individually, and then move to the closing prayer.

Close with a Prayer

Say:

- The previous exercise invited us to focus on repentance. The second command from Mark 1:15 is to believe, which is to trust in God. We will conclude this session by reading together a hymn of Charles Wesley in which he refers to the God we can trust as Love Divine.

P.23

Read together the words of Charles Wesley's hymn "Love Divine, All Loves Excelling" from the study book.

4 people

Session 2

How Can I Be Saved?

Session Summary

In this session, the authors explore what salvation means, acknowledging that when someone asks "Are you saved?" what seems a simple question can lead to some complex reflection. The Bible teaches that salvation is why God became incarnate in Jesus Christ and reveals four aspects of salvation that each help illuminate its meaning: reconciliation with God, restoration, healing, and resurrection. The apostles and the early church recognized that there was a tension within the notion of salvation regarding the necessity of faith and good works.

In his sermon "The Scripture Way of Salvation," John Wesley emphasized that both faith and good works are important for salvation. For Wesley there were two main dimensions of salvation: *justification,* which offers pardon and a change in our relationship with God, and *sanctification,* which is a process that leads to a real change in us. Faith alone is required in both of these dimensions, but good works are also necessary to continue in the journey of sanctification. Texts from Ephesians and Philippians reveal that salvation is a gift of grace and a life-long journey. Charles Wesley's hymn "And Can It Be that I Should Gain" closes the session.

Before Class

- Post a large sheet of paper or a whiteboard in a visible location for the Bible study exercise on salvation.
- Post another large sheet of paper with the following words printed on it (or write on a section of the whiteboard): reconciliation with God, restoration of broken relationships, healing, and resurrection to eternal life.
- Have available paper and drawing materials such as crayons and markers for the "Draw a House" exercise.
- Have Bibles available for group members who may not bring their own.

Welcome

Discuss What It Means to Be Saved

After everyone has arrived, say the following to the group:

- In this session we are going to be talking about what salvation means and how we can be saved. The answer to those questions is both simple and complex. To begin we are going to use our imaginations.

Ask group members to imagine that you are a stranger meeting them on the street. You are asking them a simple question: "Are you saved?" Invite volunteers from the group to share what more they would want to know before answering the question. (For example, someone might want to know whether the questioner assumes there was a special moment when that salvation happened.)

After some time for sharing, ask volunteers to answer the following question in the way they would like:

- How would you tell the story of your salvation?

Emphasize that the responses should be brief. (These are deep questions and could spawn a long discussion!)

Begin with a Prayer

Offer the following prayer or one of your own:

God of life,
We are people who often wonder,

"What will happen to me?"
We know that there are broken places in our lives
And we wonder how we can be saved.
As we meet together and search your word
Help us hear your good news in Jesus Christ
Who came to be and is our Savior. Amen.

Bible Study and Discussion

In discussing four aspects of salvation, the authors use illustrations from the Gospels where those aspects are made clear.

Begin by discussing the following question as a total group:

- What does salvation mean to you?

Write responses on a large sheet of paper or a whiteboard posted in a visible location.

Divide into four groups. Give each group one of the following passages to study:

- Luke 7:36-50: the woman anointing Jesus' feet
- Luke 19:1-10: Jesus and Zacchaeus
- Luke 18:35-43: the healing of a blind man
- John 3:16-17: "God so loved the world"

Say to the groups:

- Read your passage aloud and look for what it says about salvation. Some translations may use a word other than save or salvation, but it should be clear what kind of change the passage is talking about. Use the following questions to guide your discussion:
  ◊ What is another word for the kind of salvation being talked about in this passage?
  ◊ How does this change your understanding of what salvation is?

Come back together as a whole group. Point out the four aspects of salvation that the authors talk about, which you posted on the wall before class began: reconciliation with God, restoration of broken relationships, healing, and resurrection to eternal life. Say:

- The authors believe that the different ways that Jesus talked about salvation point to his concern for the whole person. How are these aspects still concerns for us today? What happens when we limit our understanding of salvation only to an afterlife?

Video Study and Discussion

Play the video for Session 2.

After viewing the video segment, choose some of the following questions to explore with the group:

- Do you agree with the presenters that it is more intrusive to talk about salvation than faith? Why or why not?
- If you have been baptized, what do you remember about that event or what have you been told about it? Was there a time when you felt you "owned" your baptism personally?
- What does God save us from in salvation? What are we saved for?
- How do the presenters suggest we approach talking about salvation with others?

Book Study and Discussion

Debate Faith and Good Works

Divide into two groups. Assign to one group Romans 3:28. Explain to them that this was Paul's statement in explaining how salvation was opened up to Gentiles, those who had not been subject to Jewish laws. Ask the group to develop points for why faith was an important message for Gentiles to hear and why Paul might say that justification or salvation comes "by faith apart from works" (NRSV).

Assign to the other group James 2:17. Explain that the author's concern in this passage was for the community to live out its faith in caring for those in need. Ask them to develop points for why good works are necessary for salvation.

After allowing the groups some time for discussion among themselves, have them come back together and present their points to one another debate style, with an opportunity for each group to respond to the points the other group makes.

Ask the whole group:

- What is the tension between faith and good works as a way of explaining how salvation occurs?
- How might it be possible to hold on to both understandings?

Receive a Report on Wesley's Sermon

If a volunteer has read Wesley's sermon "The Scripture Way of Salvation," invite that person to share his or her observations about the sermon. Ask him or her to address these questions: What was Wesley's central point? What were the highlights of the sermon for you?

Draw a House and Discuss Justification and Sanctification

Distribute paper and drawing utensils to the group. Invite them to sketch a house in whatever style they would like but with a porch and front door visible. After allowing some time for drawing, ask volunteers to share their sketch.

Now explain:

- In the study book, the authors refer to a metaphor that John Wesley used to describe religion. Wesley described the journey of faith as being like a house where repentance is the porch, justification is the doorway, and sanctification is the rest of the house. Let's label those parts of our drawing.

Repeat the three terms: repentance, justification, and sanctification. You may want to write them on a large sheet of paper or a whiteboard.

Say to the group:

- John Wesley believed that God's preventing or prevenient grace works in us before we are even aware in order to lead us to repentance, or a "turning around" toward God. Justification and sanctification are the two main aspects of salvation that Wesley focused on in his sermon "The Scripture Way of Salvation."

Invite the group to turn in the study book to the section "Wesley's Answer" in chapter 2. Point out the particular paragraphs where the authors discuss justification and sanctification. Using the book, ask them to find the answers to the following questions:

- How does Wesley define these two terms?
- What is the difference between them?
- How does the house metaphor help us understand that difference?

Turn Out the Lights and Discuss the Work of Salvation

If it will make the room sufficiently dark, turn out the lights for this next exercise. If turning out the lights won't make it dark enough, ask group members to close their eyes instead.

Say:

- The authors use another analogy to discuss faith. John Wesley uses Hebrews 11:1 to say that faith is "a divine evidence and conviction of things not seen." Think about the obstacles that are between you and the door right now. How would you navigate them without being able to see? How does being able to see the layout of the room help us move? If we are unable to see, we rely on senses other than sight.

Ask:

- The authors say that faith helps see what God is doing through Christ in offering salvation. How does faith impact our response?
- What does it mean that good works are necessary indirectly?

Turn on the lights (or open your eyes) at the end of this exercise.

Close the Session

Invite Someone to Read a Wesley Sermon (optional)

If you are using the option of having a volunteer read the key Wesley sermon for the following session, identify that volunteer at this point. Tell that person that you will be asking her or him to share impressions of Wesley's central point and highlights of the sermon. The sermon for the next session is "The Almost Christian."

Read Key Bible Passages as a Litany

In the section of chapter 2 titled "The Wesleyan Way of Salvation," the authors include two key Scripture passages that were important to Wesley's understanding of salvation: Ephesians 2:8-10 and Philippians 2:12-13. Have group members turn to these passages in the study book. Divide the group in half and assign one passage to each group.

Have the groups stand as they are able facing the other group. Ask them to read their passage in unison to the other group as a reminder of what God wants them to know about their salvation. When both groups have had a chance to read their passage, turn to the last exercise.

Close by Reading the Hymn

Read the history of Charles Wesley's hymn "And Can It Be that I Should Gain" from page 36 of the study book. Now ask the group, still standing, to read it aloud together. (Sing it, if you would like!)

Session 3

Am I a
Real Christian?

Session Summary

This chapter tackles the question of what it means to be an "altogether-Christian." Citing the research of Kenda Creasy Dean and Christian Smith, the authors of *Scripture and the Wesleyan Way* discuss a modern American landscape in which teenagers (and their parents) exhibit a faith that can be described as Moralistic Therapeutic Deism (MTD). MTD, with its emphasis on being nice, feeling good, and a generally absent God, leads to confusion about how Christians differ from non-Christians and anxiety about how one becomes a "real" Christian.

The authors point out that this concern is not new. Jesus talks about God's work of bringing about a wholesale transformation of the heart. The Bible talks about loving God and loving others as the means whereby we attain and enact the kingdom of God. John Wesley, in his sermon "The Almost Christian," says that Christians should expect to experience transformation in this lifetime through loving God, loving our neighbors, and having a faith that is more than belief but a trust in the power of God's love. The chapter concludes with the Charles Wesley hymn, "Come, Let Us Use the Grace Divine," which has been used by Wesleyans as part of services of recommitment.

Before Class

- Have Bibles available for group members who may not bring their own.
- On a large sheet of paper or a whiteboard that you will post in a prominent location in the meeting area, write the following quotation that is printed in chapter 3: "The opposite of love is not hate, it's indifference. The opposite of art is not ugliness, it's indifference. The opposite of faith is not heresy, it's indifference. And the opposite of life is not death, it's indifference. Because of indifference, one dies before one actually dies." —Elie Wiesel
- Post another large sheet of paper or reserve a section of the whiteboard that is easily accessible for the exercise titled "Create Tablets of the Ten Commandments." Draw two large, blank tablets (oblong boxes) side-by-side. On the first tablet, write the numbers 1–4 down the left side. On the second tablet, write the numbers 5–10.
- Post another large sheet of paper or use a third section of the whiteboard for responses to the exercise titled "Explore Moralistic Therapeutic Deism."
- Provide markers of varied colors, pencils, pens, and blank paper for use during the session.

Welcome

Consider Indifference

After welcoming group members, invite them to read aloud the Elie Wiesel quotation that you posted before the group gathered. Share with the group that Wiesel was a Jewish Holocaust survivor and writer who received the Nobel Peace Prize. Ask:

- According to this quotation, what are the things that indifference is opposed to? How healthy are these things in our world?
- Where do you see indifference in the world? in the church? in your life?

Read aloud the opening paragraph of chapter 3. Invite volunteers to share briefly a time when they experienced something like Arthur's friend did at the church concert—a time when they wondered what to do next after a powerful experience of God's presence. Ask:

- If your friend asked the same question of you, what would you tell him or her about "what to do now"?

Begin with a Prayer

Offer the following prayer or one of your own:

Loving God,
In Jesus you said that you came that we might have life and have it abundantly,
But so often we feel uncertain about what comes next
  And wonder where and how to find the abundance.
We long to leave behind indifference
  And to be fully alive.
We don't want to be "almost-Christians."
Help us to meet you and one another in this hour. Amen.

Bible Study and Discussion

Explore the Great Commandments

Ask group members to turn in their Bibles to Matthew 22:34-40. Say:

- In this section of Matthew's Gospel, Jesus is answering questions from religious groups who are trying to test him. In this passage, a questioner tries to get him to choose from among the many commands of the Law. Listen for how Jesus responds.

Invite a volunteer to read the passage. Ask other volunteers to read the passages that Jesus is referring to: Deuteronomy 6:4-5 and Leviticus 19:18. Ask:

- How does Jesus sum up the commands of the Law?
- How do the Old Testament passages help you understand what Jesus is saying?

Create Tablets of the Ten Commandments

Say to the group:

- In the section of chapter 3 titled "The Bible's Teaching," the authors talk about how the Ten Commandments of Exodus include commands to help us do both of the things Jesus talks about—love God and love neighbor. Let's see how well we remember the Ten Commandments and make two tablets—one with the commands that help us love God and the other with commands that help us love our neighbors.

Ask for a volunteer with good handwriting to go to the sheet of paper you posted before the session that has the drawing of blank tablets. Have group members call out commandments that they remember without referring to the Bible. Using the brief summary of the Ten Commandments found in *Scripture and the Wesleyan Way* (page 42), as participants call out commandments, direct the volunteer where to write them on the tablets.

If the group struggles to call out the commandments from memory, allow them to turn to Exodus 20:1-17 and find the ones that have not been called out.

Say:

- The book says that "there is a strong modern tendency to want people to be nice to their neighbor (the second tablet), but to do it without believing in God (the first tablet)."

Ask:

- How accurate do you believe this statement is? Why?
- If we took the first tablet more seriously, what would change?

Video Study and Discussion

Play the video for Session 3.

After viewing the video segment, choose some of the following questions to explore with the group:

- In this segment, Scott Jones tells the story of a truck driver who shared his faith story with him during a hitchhiking journey. When has someone related their faith to you in a way that made you think, "I want what that person has"?
  ◊ What is the difference between "Christian-ish" and "really Christian"?
  ◊ How do the authors answer the question about how we can measure our faith?

◊ How do the expectations that Jesus sets for real Christians help us grow in faith?

◊ When are the times when your church felt fully alive?

Book Study and Discussion

Explore Moralistic Therapeutic Deism

In the opening section of chapter 3, the authors discuss the writing of Kenda Creasy Dean about Moralistic Therapeutic Deism (MTD). Read aloud the paragraphs in that section related to MTD (pages 38–40). Now ask the group to define each of the elements of this type of faith:

• What makes MTD moralistic? therapeutic? deist?

As persons respond, write their answers on a large sheet of paper. Ask:

• How have you seen the MTD-type of faith in young people and in others you know? How have you seen MTD in yourself?
• Why do the authors consider that MTD could damage a "real and complete Christianity"?

Receive a Report on Wesley's Sermon

If a volunteer has read the Wesley sermon "The Almost Christian," invite that person to share his or her observations about the sermon. Ask him or her to address these questions:

• What was Wesley's central point?
• What were the highlights of the sermon for you?

Discuss Wesley's View of the Altogether-Christian

In the section of chapter 3 titled "Wesley's Answer," the authors discuss how Wesley made his movement from being an almost-Christian to an altogether-Christian. Read aloud the paragraphs in this section that describe Wesley's personal experience of having his heart "strangely warmed." [These are the two paragraphs beginning with "You might be thinking, what is wrong with this?" on pages 45–46.]

Say:

- Wesley's sermon highlights three changes that accompany becoming an altogether-Christian—loving God, loving our neighbor, and having faith.

Divide into three groups and assign each group one of the changes Wesley talks about. Have them review the paragraph in the book related to their assigned topic (see pages 46–47). Ask them to use the following questions to guide their small group discussion:

- How does Wesley describe this change?
- What is surprising or unusual about Wesley's understanding of this change?

When you gather as a total group, have each small group briefly present their responses to the questions.

Create a Word Cloud of the Almost- and the Altogether-Christian

Distribute paper and writing instruments to group members. Ask them to write the word "ALMOST" in block letters in the center of a blank sheet of paper. On the back of that page, have them write "ALTOGETHER" in block letters in the center.

Say:

- Now that we have had some time to discuss what John Wesley meant by "almost" and "altogether," let's capture some words that we associate with these concepts by making a word cloud for each one. For instance, we might think "dutiful" is an appropriate word for an almost-Christian, so we write that near the word "ALMOST." For an altogether-Christian, we might think "alive" is appropriate. Brainstorm and create a cloud of words on both sides of the paper.

After allowing some time for individual work, invite volunteers to share their word clouds with the whole group.

Explore the Importance of the Altogether-Christian Life

The authors begin the section of chapter 3 titled "The Wesleyan Way of Salvation" with a paragraph that describes why the altogether Christian life is important. Read that paragraph aloud on page 48 and discuss the following questions:

- Why is an altogether Christian life important for us?
- Why is it important for others?

Close the Session

Invite Someone to Read a Wesley Sermon (optional)

If you are using the option of having a volunteer read the key Wesley sermon for the following session, identify that volunteer at this point. Because there are two sermons for the next session, you could have two volunteers. Tell the reader(s) that you will be asking for impressions of Wesley's central point and highlights of the sermons. The sermons for the next session are "The Law Established Through Faith, I and II."

Reflect on Wesley's Self-examination Questions:

Say:

- John Wesley felt that Christians should expect that transformation is possible in this lifetime because of God's power. Wesley's understanding of sanctification led him to believe that we can experience salvation not just after this life, but now. In the sermon "The Almost Christian," he includes a series of questions to help us examine how strongly we are experiencing the love of God and to inspire us to draw closer to God. The self-examination questions are found in the quotation from Wesley at the end of the section titled "Wesley's Answer" in chapter 3 (page 47). As I read this paragraph of questions aloud, follow along or close your eyes and listen. Consider silently how you would honestly answer Wesley's questions.

Read the paragraph from the book, pausing after each question for a few seconds. Close by saying:

- God's love is powerful. God loves you. You were made to be a child of God.

Close by Reading the Hymn

Read the introduction to Charles Wesley's hymn "Come, Let Us Use the Grace Divine" from the study book. Now ask the group to read it aloud together. (Or sing!)

Do I Have to Obey the Law?

Session Summary

In chapter 4, the authors address the role of the Law in Christian life and how it relates to grace. While some churches emphasize obedience to rules to the exclusion of forgiveness and grace, others do exactly the reverse. A biblical and Wesleyan understanding reveals that law and grace have always been found together and each is an aspect of God's work of salvation.

The authors use two of John Wesley's sermons, "The Law Established Through Faith, I and II," to explore how Wesley saw this interrelationship. In this session, we will explore the biblical roots of a Christian understanding of the Law, including the description of the Jerusalem Council in Acts 15, which eventually led to an important distinction among the different types of law found in the Old Testament: ceremonial, civil, and moral laws. John Wesley upheld the continuing relevance of the moral law as an instrument to convince us of sin, to bring us to life in Christ, and to keep us alive by drawing us continually back to Christ. The session includes reflections on the role of perfection in "The Wesleyan Way of Salvation."

Before Class

- Have Bibles available for group members who may not bring their own.
- Provide markers of varied colors, pencils, pens, and blank paper for use during the session.
- On a large sheet of paper or a section of the whiteboard, write the words "The Wesleyan Way of Salvation" across the top. Then write the following questions with plenty of space after each for writing responses:
  ◊ What Is the Bible's Message?
  ◊ How Can I Be Saved?
  ◊ How Do I Know If I Am a Real Christian?
  ◊ Do I Have to Obey the Law?
- Post another large sheet of paper or use another section of the whiteboard for the exercise titled "Share Rules of the House."

Welcome

Review Previous Lessons

After participants have arrived, say:

- In this study we have been exploring how John Wesley looked at Scripture to answer big spiritual questions that still matter to us today. We have been looking at individual questions, but you may have noticed how the answers build on each other. We can start to build a picture of how the Wesleys viewed salvation by reviewing where we've been.

Invite group members to share their recollections of the previous sessions by asking the featured question of each one and discussing how John Wesley and the Bible answered each. After the group shares responses to each question, write the sentence suggested below underneath the questions you pre-printed on a large sheet of paper and posted before the session.

1. What Is the Bible's Message?

Write on the sheet: "The Bible's central message is the kingdom of God, which is marked by righteousness, peace, and joy. We experience it through repentance and faith."

2. How Can I Be Saved?

Write on the sheet: "Salvation is a present and future reality. We experience it through justification, which changes our relationship with God, and sanctification, which is a process of transformation in us. Salvation comes through faith alone but results in good works."

3. How Do I Know If I Am a Real Christian?

Write on the sheet: "Sanctification includes the expectation that we can experience salvation now through loving God and loving others, as expressed in Jesus' Great Commandment."

Say to the group:

- You may notice that some words keep popping up as we answer these questions. Some key ones that we've talked about are—repentance, justification, and sanctification. *[Underline these words on the posted paper.]* As we look at today's question, we will see these words again and add another important one. These words help define a Wesleyan Way of Salvation.

Begin with a Prayer

Offer the following prayer or one of your own:

Christ, who is the Way, the Truth, and the Life,
We want to follow where you lead.
We want to experience the joy of your salvation
And to live by the power of your love.
Help us see you in our gathering today. Amen.

Bible Study and Discussion

Discuss Grace and Law in the Bible

Say to the group:

- In the section of chapter 4 titled "The Bible's Teaching," the authors talk about the role of the Law and how it is understood throughout the Bible.

We are going to take a look at several different paragraphs from this section to look at the progression of that story.

Divide into four groups. Assign each group one of the following perspectives to explore: **Jewish Law** (the first three paragraphs of the section, page 53), **the Prophets** (paragraphs four and five, including the text of Isaiah 1:11-20, pages 54–55), **Jesus** (the two paragraphs following the discussion of the prophets, beginning "Jesus' preaching about the kingdom of God," including the text of Matthew 23:23-24, pages 55–56), and **Paul and James** (the two paragraphs following the discussion of Jesus, page 57).

Ask the groups to use the following questions in exploring their assigned perspective:

- What does this part of the Bible say about the role of the Law?
- How does this perspective also include forgiveness and/or grace?

After some time for small group discussion, come back together and have each group report on what they found.

Simulate the Jerusalem Council

Ask for five volunteers to help simulate the Jerusalem Council described in Acts 15:1-21. Explain that this conference was a critical moment in the Christian understanding of the Law. Identify the following roles of the volunteers: Narrator, Peter, Barnabas, Paul, and James. Tell the rest of the group to imagine that they are the other apostles and elders who attended the council.

Have the narrator stand and read *slowly* Acts 15:1-5 and then all of the parts of Acts 15:6-21 that are not dialogue. Invite group members to follow along in their own Bibles. Explain that beginning with verse 6, you will be simulating the Jerusalem Council. Paul and Barnabas do not have speaking roles, but they should mime the actions described. Peter should read the dialogue in verses 7-11. James should read the dialogue in verses 13-21.

After the simulation, discuss the following questions:

- How did taking the gospel to other nations (Gentiles) affect the apostles' understanding of the Law?
- How does Peter say the Gentiles will be saved in verse 11?
- What parts of the Law were the Gentiles asked to keep?

Video Study and Discussion

Play the video for Session 4.

After viewing the video segment, choose some of the following questions to explore with the group:

- What is the relationship between the Old Testament and New Testament? Where do we see continuity and where do we see change?
- Jameson's friend told him that he wished his parents loved him enough to place rules on him. How does this statement show us the purpose of God's rules?
- What do the authors mean by perfection? How does it relate to obedience?
- Who has been an Elizabeth Snell—a saint—in your life? What do you admire about him or her?

Book Study and Discussion

Receive a Report on Wesley's Sermon

If a volunteer or volunteers have read Wesley's sermons "The Law Established Through Faith, I and II," invite those persons to share briefly their observations about the sermons. Ask them to address these questions:

- What was Wesley's central point?
- What were the highlights of the sermon for you?

Share Rules of the House

Ask group members to reflect on the rules they grew up with in their home or the rules that they have in their current homes. Have them name a few. Ask:

- What purpose did those rules serve?
- How did they keep you out of trouble?
- How did they help maintain good relationships in the house?

Say to the group:

- Just like the Anglican Church of which he was a part, John Wesley believed that there were three types of Old Testament Law: the ceremonial, the civil, and the moral law. After Jesus' death and resurrection, the moral law is still binding for Christians.

Invite class members to turn to the section of chapter 4 titled, "Wesley's Answer" (page 58) to find answers to the following question. Ask:

What are the three ways the moral law still functions in bringing us to salvation?

Write the responses on a large sheet of paper that you posted before the session began: [1) convinces us of sin, 2) brings us to life in Christ, 3) keeps us alive].

If you used the house drawing exercise in Session 2, remind the group of Wesley's analogy of the house to explain salvation. [Repeat the exercise if you like.] Remind them that the porch represents prevenient grace and repentance, the door is justification, and the interior of the house is sanctification. Ask:

How do the three functions of the moral law relate to the image of the house?
How does the law act like the "house rules" in your home?

Consider "Walking the Walk"

In the last few paragraphs of the section entitled "Wesley's Answer," the authors describe what Wesley meant by establishing the law (page 62). Invite the group to turn to this section as you ask the following questions:

- What does Wesley mean by establishing the law in our hearts and lives?
- How does "walking the walk" help us live out of God's law and grace?

Attempt Perfection

Invite a volunteer to share a time when he or she has seen someone attain a level of perfection. For example, a pitcher throwing a perfect game in baseball or a host laying out a perfect meal for guests. Ask:

- Why do we remember such moments?
- Why does perfection seem unattainable for us?

Refer to the section of chapter 4 titled, "The Wesleyan Way of Salvation" (page 63) to answer the next questions. Read aloud the last five paragraphs of the section starting with the paragraph that begins "Perfection for Wesley..." Ask:

- How does Wesley's definition of perfection differ from how we usually think about it?
- How does having a goal of perfection affect our understanding of the moral law?
- How would our churches change if we took this understanding seriously?

Close the Session

Invite Someone to Read a Wesley Sermon (optional)

If you are using the option of having a volunteer read the key Wesley sermon for the following session, identify that volunteer at this point. Tell that person that you will be asking her or him to share impressions of Wesley's central point and highlights of the sermon. The sermon for the next session is "Original Sin."

Review "The Wesleyan Way of Salvation"

Direct the group's attention to the sheet you posted earlier titled "The Wesleyan Way of Salvation." Ask the group to discuss what Wesley's response to the fourth question would be. Write the suggested words below on the paper.

4. Do I Have to Obey the Law?

Write on the sheet: "We are saved by grace through faith, but sanctification is a lifelong journey and the moral law has a role as it draws us toward perfection."

Underline the words *sanctification* and *perfection*. Say:

- We have added a new word to our Wesleyan vocabulary today—perfection. Most of us are hesitant to use this word to describe the Christian life, but it should be our goal. The Law helps move us toward this goal.

Retain this sheet for use in future sessions.

Close with a Hymn

Introduce the Charles Wesley hymn "A Charge to Keep I Have" as a prayer that also reminds us of the importance of Christian commitment to receive God's grace so that we can fulfill God's intentions for us as we grow toward perfection.

Read or sing the hymn together as it is printed in the study book (page 66).

Session 5

Am I a Sinner?

Session Summary

In this session, the authors look at the question of sin and brokenness and how it continues to impact our lives even if we are uncomfortable talking about it in the modern age. After addressing how our society thinks about self-esteem today, the authors return to a long-held doctrine of the church—original sin—and discuss how ignoring the brokenness in our lives leaves us with an incomplete picture of ourselves. The Bible paints a realistic picture of human nature and the way that grace addresses the problem of sin.

John Wesley's sermon "Original Sin" addresses a necessary starting point for understanding salvation: Proper religion means acknowledging that we can't heal ourselves. We all are sinners, but we have a Great Physician in Jesus who offers us forgiveness and healing as a way to deal with sin. When we acknowledge our own inability to save ourselves and turn to God, we trust in God's grace to heal us. John Newton's familiar song, "Amazing Grace," closes the chapter.

Before Class

- Have Bibles available for group members who may not bring their own.
- Provide markers of varied colors, pencils, pens, and blank paper for use during the session.

- Post the sheet titled "The Wesleyan Way of Salvation" that you created in the last session in a visible place in the room.
- Post another large sheet of paper for the exercise titled "Review the Wesleyan Way of Salvation" or plan to use a section of a whiteboard for this purpose.
- If you are using the optional exercise for Mr. Rogers, arrange to have a monitor or projector and a computer to show the video clip of "Sometimes People Are Right." It can be found on YouTube at: **http://tiny.cc/m8yguy** (this should point to https://www.youtube.com /watch?v=11HOw5oorDc&index=7&t=0s&list=PLmnFhtOlK0 _uiwB0bOSM2SFvdMAuY9jHR). The lyrics are also available at this site: http://www.neighborhoodarchive.com/music/songs/sometimes_people _are_good.html.

Welcome

Remember Mr. Rogers

After participants arrive, ask how many people in the group are familiar with Mr. Rogers, the television presenter mentioned in the opening paragraphs of chapter 5 of *Scripture and the Wesleyan Way*. If there are some people who are familiar with Mr. Rogers' show, invite them to share their memories of the show:

- What were some of Mr. Rogers' routines?
- How did he speak to children? How did he make you feel?
- What were some of his major themes?

Read aloud the two paragraphs in the opening section related to him (pages 68–69). Ask:

- According to the authors, how did Mr. Rogers help children know they have value and are loved?
- How did Mr. Rogers help children hear other messages about themselves?

[*Optional exercise*: Show a video clip of *Mr. Rogers' Neighborhood*. One song that shows Mr. Rogers' ability to convey the complexity of human nature is "Sometimes People Are Right." A link to the clip and another to the lyrics can be found above in the "Before Class" section.]

Ask:

- How is self-esteem important to children (and adults)?
- Why do we also need to hear that we are, as Brené Brown says, "imperfect" and "wired for struggle"?

Open with a Prayer

Use the opening prayer or one of your own:

Loving God,

It is easy for us to acknowledge that everything is not OK.

We can look within our lives, our families, our communities, and our world

and we see the ways we are not what you or even Mr. Rogers

believes we can be.

We want to be made whole.

We want to understand what it means to be your creatures and your children.

Come help us hear who we are in your eyes. Amen.

Bible Study and Discussion

Revisit the Story of Noah and His Family

Say to the group:

- The Bible presents us with a very realistic portrait of who we are. In "The Bible's Teaching" section of chapter 5, we read a number of passages that reveal how sin distorts our lives. Let's revisit one of those stories—the story of God and Noah and his family.

Ask:

- What images do you remember from the Noah story?

[*Participants might mention visuals such as the ark, the animals, the Flood, the dove, the rainbow, and so on.*]

Invite a volunteer to tell the story of Noah as if she or he were sharing it with children. Ask:

- What are the things we want children to hear about the story?

Now divide into three groups. Have each group look at a different part of the Noah story:

Read

- Why God sent the Flood—Genesis 6:5-8
- God's promise after the Flood—Genesis 8:20-22
- God's covenant with all creatures—Genesis 9:8-17

After allowing the groups to talk briefly about the central message of their assigned passage, gather again as a large group. Ask:

- What do these passages tell us about human beings?
- What do these passages tell us about God?
- Where do you see sin and promise in this story?

(4) ***Explore the Enduring Power of Sin***

Say to the group:

- Paul writes in the Book of Romans that sin is more than just actions that we do. He describes an internal struggle against a power that works against him.

Invite a volunteer to read aloud Romans 7:15-25. Ask:

- What is Paul's struggle?
- How have you experienced this same struggle in your own life?
- What does this struggle suggest about the nature of sin?
- Why is Paul able to give thanks at the end of this passage?

Video Study and Discussion

Play the video for Session 5.

After viewing the video segment, choose some of the following questions to explore with the group:

- Tell a brief story of when you first became aware of brokenness and sin in the world.
- According to the authors, why are prayers of confession so crucial for us as human beings?
- How is John Newton's story of redemption through God's grace our story?
- What are some of the ways that the presenters offer for helping us accept forgiveness ourselves? What others would you add?

Book Study and Discussion

Receive a Report on Wesley's Sermon

If a volunteer has read the Wesley sermon "Original Sin," invite that person to share his or her observations about the sermon. Ask him or her to address these questions:

- What was Wesley's central point?
- What were the highlights of the sermon for you?

Imagine a Conversation with a Non-Christian

Say:

- The authors of the study book begin chapter 5 by discussing how some of us resist talking about sin despite the fact that most of us acknowledge that we are broken.

Ask:

- Why do you believe it is difficult for us to talk about brokenness and sin?
- Do you agree with the authors' assertion that we just want to feel good? Why or why not?

Read aloud (or have a volunteer read) the first three paragraphs of the "Wesley's Answer" section of chapter 5 (pages 74–75). Ask:

- Why is the concept of original sin "the foundation of Christian wisdom"?
- What is the danger in thinking that "we are partially broken"?

Distribute paper and drawing utensils to group members. Say:

- Imagine that you have been charged with building an ad campaign to describe original sin to a general (non-Christian) audience. How would you communicate Wesley's message to persons who do not want to consider sin? What is the good news that Wesley wants to communicate?

After allowing several minutes for individual work, invite volunteers to share their ads with the group.

Consider the Image of the Great Physician

Read aloud (or have a volunteer read) the final two paragraphs of the "Wesley's Answer" section of chapter 5 (pages 75–76). Say:

- John Wesley uses the image of the great physician to describe how God addresses human brokenness. Other images that have been used to describe Jesus' role are judge, good shepherd, and high priest.

Ask:

- What does the image of Jesus as Great Physician tell us about how God views sin?
- What is the relation of a patient to a physician?
- How is sin like a wound or disease?
- What is the role of grace, according to Wesley?

 ### Review "The Wesleyan Way of Salvation"

In the previous chapter (chapter 4), in the section titled "The Wesleyan Way of Salvation," the authors list five terms. Invite group members to turn to this section of the book (page 64) and call out these five terms of the way of salvation as you (or a volunteer) write them on a large sheet of paper: *Creation in the image of God, Sin, Repentance, Justification, Sanctification.*

Ask:

- What role does sin play in the story of salvation?
- What would happen if God did not address the problem of brokenness and sin?

- In chapter 5, the authors say that Jesus' work in justification is to forgive us and his work in sanctification is to heal us. How does this distinction help us understand what grace does?

Invite a volunteer to tell a story using these five terms. Make God the main actor in the story. What is God's role in creating, dealing with sin, and restoring the relationship of humanity with God?

Close the Session

Invite Someone to Read a Wesley Sermon (optional)

If you are using the option of having a volunteer read the key Wesley sermon for the following session, identify that volunteer at this point. Tell that person that you will be asking her or him to share impressions of Wesley's central point and highlights of the sermon. The sermon for the next session is "The Means of Grace."

Envision the Church as Midwife

Read aloud (or have a volunteer read) the final paragraph of the section "The Wesleyan Way of Salvation" in chapter 5 (page 77). Ask:

- What does Brené Brown mean by saying that church is not an epidural, but a midwife?
- Why is it important that the church allow space for "acknowledging our brokenness and total corruption"?

Ask group members to consider how their church or community of faith allows members to confront their own brokenness. Review worship, small group, and other ministries with this question in mind. Allow a few minutes for individual reflection. Then ask:

- What are the spaces where you feel free and safe to share your own brokenness?
- What opportunities do we have to extend this space in our life together?
- What is the danger of believing that we do not need healing?

Close with a Hymn

Read the introduction to "Amazing Grace" near the end of chapter 5. Invite the group to sing the hymn together, reading from the book.

Session 6

How Can I Connect with God?

Session Summary

Chapter 6 addresses the question of how we can maintain and grow in our connection to God. The authors describe the biblical history of a loving God reaching out to humanity in order to save it. In the Old Testament, God responds to the ongoing disobedience of human beings by creating a covenant with a particular people, Israel, and establishing commandments, structure, and worship practices that helped the people draw near to God. In the Christian church, two particular ceremonies commanded by Jesus—baptism and Holy Communion—became sacraments.

John Wesley's sermon "The Means of Grace" builds on this biblical history to describe Christian practices that reliably connect us with God's grace. In the sermon, Wesley lists three means of grace: prayer, searching the Scriptures, and the Lord's Supper. In other writings, he talks about fasting and Christian conferencing as well. These practices are not the goal of the Christian life, but a means of staying in touch with the transformative power of God's love. Charles Wesley's hymn "Come, Sinners, to the Gospel Feast" concludes the chapter and serves as an invitation to seeing Holy Communion as a powerful means of grace.

Before Class

Prepare a table in the middle of your meeting space as a worship center. On the table, place some visible reminders of the means of grace that you will be talking about during the session. Be sure to place a basin of water in the display for use during the closing exercise. Other objects you can include: an open Bible, a pitcher, a chalice, a loaf of bread, a prayer book.

- Have Bibles available for group members who may not bring their own.
- Provide markers of varied colors, pencils, pens, and blank paper for use during the session.
- Post the sheet titled "The Wesleyan Way of Salvation" that you created in a previous session in a visible place in the room.
- On another large sheet of paper (or part of a whiteboard) write the words "The Means of Grace." Beneath this write this sentence from *Scripture and the Wesleyan Way*: "The goal of all Christian practices is a transformed heart—one that loves God fully and loves one's neighbor as oneself."
- Post another large sheet of paper horizontally (landscape mode) for the exercise titled "Means of Grace Check-Up," or use another section of the whiteboard for this exercise.

Welcome

Consider How to Maintain Relationships

After the group arrives, explain that the focus of the session today will be on the means of grace, which are ways to help us maintain and strengthen our connection to God. Say:

- Before we turn to our relationship with God, let's think about how we maintain and strengthen our other relationships. Close your eyes and think about a relationship that is significant to you. Perhaps it is your relationship with a spouse, a parent, a friend, or even a pet.

After some moments for individual reflection, have participants open their eyes again. Ask:

- What are the things you do that help you stay close to the other partner in the relationship?
- How is maintaining your relationship with God like this relationship?
- What's different?

Now direct the group's attention to the large sheet of paper you posted before the session that begins with the title "The Means of Grace." Read it aloud together.

Ask:

- How does this statement help us understand the purpose of the means of grace?

Begin with a Prayer

Offer the following prayer or one of your own:

Loving God,
The Scriptures say that when we draw near to you,
  You draw near to us.
We have trouble staying close.
We admit that often we are distracted, anxious, and alone.
We want a vital relationship with you
  and a transformed heart.
We draw near to one another in this hour,
  and we draw near to you.
Come meet us, Lord. Amen.

Bible Study and Discussion

Asking for Help

Say to the group:

- In the opening paragraphs of chapter 6, the authors say that "human beings are in spiritual danger" and that the first step toward salvation is recognizing that we have a problem. The second step, they say, is to find help, and God is the source of that help.

#2 Ask participants to think about how they generally seek help when they recognize they are in trouble. Ask:

- Where do you turn for help?
- Why is it difficult for us to admit that we need help?
- What do people do who are seeking God's help?
- Why is it difficult for us to admit that we are helpless to save ourselves?

Explore the Sacraments

Say to the group:

#3
- In "The Bible's Teaching" section of chapter 6, we read how the Bible is the story of God acting to save the world. Throughout Israel's history, God offers the people ways to connect to God.

Invite the group to turn to this section of the book on pages 80–85 and to skim it as you ask the following questions:

- What are some of the ways God offers Israel to connect with God? [*Possible answers include: the covenant with Abraham and Sarah, laws, commandments, sanctuaries, the temple, synagogues, and worship.*]
- Which two ceremonies became central to Christian worship? [*Baptism and Holy Communion*]

Say:

- Baptism and Communion are sacraments—outward and visible signs of an inward and spiritual grace. Let's explore what the Bible says about them.

#1 Divide into two groups. Have one group explore baptism using Galatians 3:26-29. Ask the other group to use 1 Corinthians 11:23-26 to explore Communion. Have them *#2* use the following questions to guide their discussion:

Ask #1
- What does this passage tell us about how the sacrament connects us to Christ?

#2 • How have you felt connected to Christ through participating in these sacraments?

Come together as a large group to briefly share observations and insights from the small group discussion.

Video Study and Discussion

Play the video for Session 6.

After viewing the video segment, choose some of the following questions to explore with the group:

- Why is it important not to put our feelings on a pedestal?
- How can our attitude affect our experience of church or other spiritual practices?
- How do you set priorities that help you connect with God regularly?
- If you have a strong sense of connection to God, how would you describe it to someone else?

Book Study and Discussion

Receive a Report on Wesley's Sermon

If a volunteer has read the Wesley sermon "The Means of Grace," invite that person to share his or her observations about the sermon. Ask that person to address these questions:

- What was Wesley's central point?
- What were the highlights of the sermon for you?

Do a Means of Grace Check-up:

Say to the group:

- Most of us would like to have a stronger experience of the means of grace than we currently have. John Wesley and the small groups of Methodists he developed regularly examined their spiritual lives to see how they were pursuing greater spiritual transformation. Let's do a spiritual check-up with the means of grace to see how we're doing.

Do This

Distribute blank pieces of paper and writing instruments to group members. As you offer directions for this exercise, demonstrate the steps by making a model on a large sheet of paper on the wall. Ask the group to turn the paper with the long side at the top (landscape mode), and make a grid with 5 columns and 6 rows, leaving plenty of room to write in each resulting cell. [*Draw this grid on the large sheet of paper.*]

Then, have the participants write the following column headings along the top row of the grid: *Means of Grace, Questions, Scripture, Current Practice, Next Step.*

Now, ask the group to write the following means of grace, which are discussed in chapter 6, in the remaining rows of the left-most column: *Prayer, Bible reading, Communion, Fasting, Conferencing.*

Ask the group to now fill in the grid based on their experience of these means of grace and the reading in chapter 6, (primarily the "Wesley's Answer" section on pages 85–90). In the Questions column, invite them to jot down any questions they have about the practice. What more would they like to know?

Under the Scripture heading, ask them to write down Scripture references from the book related to this practice. Two of the means of grace have no Scripture verse mentioned. Invite the group to write Matthew 6:16-18 in the cell by fasting and Acts 2:42-46 in the cell by conferencing.

In the Current Practice column, note what you are currently doing in this area. And in the final column, set an intention of one thing you can do as a next step in this practice.

Allow the group some time to work on this project individually. When you gather back together, ask for insights and encourage participants to find small groups (or create one) in which they can pursue growth in the means of grace together.

Return to Arthur's Friend

In the section titled "The Wesleyan Way of Salvation," the authors return to the story of Arthur's friend who wondered "What do I do now?" after a powerful experience at a Christian concert. Read aloud the concluding paragraphs of this section where the authors offer a possible response to that question (page 91).

Ask the group:

- What does this response tell us about the form of the Christian life?
- How do we stay focused on the goal of discipleship and not merely the means?
- What is God doing as we attend to the means of grace?

Close the Session

Invite Someone to Read a Wesley Sermon (optional)

If you are using the option of having a volunteer read the key Wesley sermon for the following session, identify that volunteer at this point. Tell that person that you will be asking her or him to share impressions of Wesley's central point and highlights of the sermon. The sermon for the next session is "The Repentance of Believers."

Remember Your Baptism

Direct group members' attention to the bowl of water you placed in the worship center before the session began. Say:

- In the Methodist tradition, baptism can happen at any stage of life and it is not repeated. But we can recall our baptisms frequently and be reminded of God's promise over our lives. We have a bowl of water here as a reminder of God's gift of baptism. You are invited to come and dip a finger in the water to remember your baptism, if you have been baptized, or to give thanks for God's reaching out to us with grace. You can make the sign of the cross on your forehead with the water.

After all the participants who desire to do so have come forward, place your hand in the bowl and cup a handful of water. Raise your hand dramatically and let the water fall back to the bowl. As you do, look at the participants and say:

- Remember your baptism and be thankful!

If there are any persons who have not been baptized but who express a desire to be baptized, connect them with the pastor or other leader of your community of faith following the session.

Close with a Hymn

Introduce the hymn "Come, Sinners, to the Gospel Feast" and share that Charles Wesley wrote it as an invitation to experience God's grace through Holy Communion. Ask participants to pay particular attention to what God and Jesus are offering in this hymn. Then read (or sing) the hymn together.

Session 7

Why Is the Christian Life So Hard?

Session Summary

Chapter 7 introduces the concept of the "holiness gap"—the gap we feel between the expectations of the holy life and our actual lives. How do we understand the continuing struggles of the Christian life, which we experience even after coming to faith? In this session we explore how the biblical and Wesleyan notion of repentance sheds light on the continuing journey of believers.

The Bible's central message, as we learned in Session 1, is the kingdom of God, but it also tells the story of how this kingdom should be made real in our lives. Repentance is the crucial response to the revelation of God's intentions. It is a complete transformation of our hearts and a return to who we are supposed to be.

John Wesley's sermon "The Repentance of Believers" talks about the way that sin remains in the believer's life, even after justification. Through continuing repentance, believers can experience real, inward change and move toward holiness. The chapter concludes with Charles Wesley's hymn "Depth of Mercy," which describes the story of repentance.

Before Class

- Have Bibles available for group members who may not bring their own.
- Provide markers of varied colors, pencils, pens, and blank paper for use during the session.
- Arrange the room for a maximum amount of open space to allow for the movement in the opening exercise, the *Shub* game. You may want to identify a larger space you can use or consider going outside for that activity.
- Post the sheet titled "The Wesleyan Way of Salvation" that you created in a previous session in a visible place in the room.
- Prepare a second sheet to post next to "The Wesleyan Way of Salvation" sheet (or plan to use part of the whiteboard). Write the following questions on it, leaving plenty of space after each question for writing responses. Also leave space for an additional question and response in the next session.
  1. Am I a Sinner?
  2. How Can I Connect with God?
  3. Why Is Christian Life So Hard?

Welcome

Play a Game of Shub

After participants have arrived, explain that you are going to begin with a game of *Shub*. Explain that the word *shub* is introduced in "The Bible's Teaching" section of chapter 7 as an Old Testament word for "repentance." Read aloud the paragraph from this section on page 96 that describes the concept as it is found in the Book of Jonah. (The paragraph begins, "In the Old Testament, the Hebrew word...")

Explain the rules of Shub:

- Get a partner and then find a spot in the room that you will call home base. When I call "Go," one person in your pair should wander away from your partner. Take your time as you walk, noticing the room and the other people you meet. When I call "Shub," move quickly back to home base and high-five your partner. (Running and/or knocking over furniture is not allowed.) The first pair to high-five at their home base will be considered the winners of the round.

After a few rounds of *Shub*, have everyone return to their seats. Discuss:

- How does this game help us understand the concept of repentance?
- If the partner who stays at home base in the game represents God, what does this suggest about the relationship between God and humanity?

[You may need to adapt this game if there are group members with mobility issues.]

Begin with a Prayer

God of New Beginnings,
  You call us to shub, to return from the many ways we turn from you
    and you call us to walk with you.
We long to be the people you intend us to be
  But we recognize the struggles still within us
    and the sin that clings so closely.
Help us turn to you and receive the grace you offer freely;
  in Jesus Christ. Amen.

Bible Study and Discussion

Paraphrase Psalm 51

In "The Bible's Teaching" section of chapter 7, the authors lift up Psalm 51 as a psalm of repentance (see pages 98–99). Read aloud the paragraph relating to Psalm 51 from the book. (The paragraph begins, "The Bible also depicts repentance on a personal level.")

Say to the group members:

- Psalm 51 gives us a model of what a prayer of repentance looks like. One way to hear the psalm with fresh ears is to put it into your own words.

Distribute blank pieces of paper, pens, pencils, and other drawing utensils to participants. Invite them to read Psalm 51:7-10 from the Bible silently. Then, ask them to spend a few minutes rewriting the verses in their own words. For some, it may be more useful to them to do a drawing that depicts what they hear in the verses.

After participants have had some time to do the exercise, invite volunteers to share their work. Ask:

- How does this exercise help you understand the desire to be whole?
- How can repentance lead to joy?

Consider a Heart Transplant

Have a volunteer read aloud Ezekiel 36:26 from the Bible. Ask:

- What is the promise in this verse?
- Why do human beings need a new heart in order to be close to God?

Divide into small groups of three or four people. Invite each group to look at the same two passages: Matthew 5:21-22 and Matthew 5:27-28. Ask them to read the passages and then discuss them using the following questions:

- What is Jesus saying here?
- What would have to happen in order for us to fulfill these commands?

Come back together as total group. Ask:

- How do Jesus' standards help us understand the necessity of repentance?

Video Study and Discussion

Play the video for Session 7.

After viewing the video segment, choose some of the following questions to explore with the group:

- How does the analogy of living into marriage vows help us understand the journey of the Christian life?
- How do the authors answer the question of whether we can "lose" God's grace?
- Tell a story about a time when doing the hard things led to a better life for you.
- What are the things that make you complacent about your faith?

Book Study and Discussion

Mind the Holiness Gap

Invite group members to recall a recent TV show or movie they have seen that included an identifiable Christian character. Ask:

- How was this Christian character portrayed?
- What does this portrayal say about how Christians are viewed in the larger world?

Now read aloud the first two paragraphs of chapter 7, in which the authors discuss the gap "between the example of Jesus and those who follow Jesus" (page 93). Ask:

- Where do you see an awareness of this gap in the world? in your circle of friends?

Read the quotation from Brennan Manning from the next paragraph (on page 94): "The greatest single cause of atheism in the world today is Christians who acknowledge Jesus with their lips then walk out the door and deny him by their lifestyle. That is what an unbelieving world simply finds unbelievable." Ask:

- Do you agree with this statement? Why or why not?
- What is the cause of the gap between what Christians profess and how we live?

Receive a Report on Wesley's Sermon

If a volunteer has read the Wesley sermon "The Repentance of Believers," invite that person to share her or his observations about the sermon. Ask the volunteer reader to address these questions:

- What was Wesley's central point?
- What were the highlights of the sermon for you?

Return to "The Wesleyan Way of Salvation"

Direct the group's attention to the sheet titled "The Wesleyan Way of Salvation" that you created for Session 4. On a second sheet that is posted by it, invite the group to review the last two sessions in a similar way. Read the questions for Sessions 5 and 6, discuss how the Bible and John Wesley answered them, and then write the following suggested words beneath each question.

5. *Am I a Sinner?*

Write on the sheet: "We all are impacted by the power of sin and are unable to save ourselves. Jesus the Great Physician forgives and heals that sin."

6. *How Can I Connect with God?*

Write on the sheet: "God provides us with the means of grace to help us maintain and grow in our connection to God. Among these are prayer, Bible reading, Holy Communion, fasting, and Christian conferencing."

Underline the words *sin* and *grace*. Invite the group to consider how the underlined words from the previous six sessions play a role in the Wesleyan Way of Salvation. Spend some time with each of the following words: *sin, grace, justification, sanctification,* and *perfection.*

Say to the group:

- Repentance is a word that we underlined from the first session. We have talked about how repentance is necessary to enter the Christian journey and how it accompanies justification. In this session we also learned why repentance is part of the life of believers who want to experience a real change in their lives.

Point to the question for chapter 7 on the sheet and invite group members to reflect on how the Bible and Wesley answer it. Then write the following suggested words below the question.

7. *Why Is Christian Life So Hard?*

Write on the sheet: "Repentance is not only a turning back to God but a complete transformation of our hearts. Believers can experience real, inward change, but only through ongoing repentance."

Underline the word *repentance*. Ask:

- How is repentance part of God's good news?

Close the Session

Invite Someone to Read a Wesley Sermon (optional)

If you are using the option of having a volunteer read the key Wesley sermon for the following session, identify that volunteer at this point. Tell that person that you will be asking her or him to share impressions of Wesley's central point and highlights of the sermon. The sermon for the next session is "The Use of Money."

Pray the Covenant Prayer Together

Have participants turn to "The Wesleyan Way of Salvation" section of chapter 7 (page 104). Read aloud (or have a volunteer read) this section.

Now, invite group members to consider the words of Wesley's Covenant Prayer, (pages 105–106) which is included in this section. Ask them to consider the following questions as they silently read through the prayer:

- What would it mean for my life if I took this prayer seriously?
- What areas of my life require a deeper repentance?

After some moments for individual reflection, ask the group to join you in reciting the prayer. Acknowledge that, given the radical commitment of the prayer, some participants may decide to listen as others read.

Read a Hymn to Close

Close by reading together (or singing) Charles Wesley's hymn "Depth of Mercy."

Session 8

What About My Money?

Session Summary

In the final chapter of *Scripture and the Wesleyan Way*, the authors turn to the question of money and how we use it. While people are often reluctant to talk about money, our approach to finances reveals a lot about where our heart is. The biblical witness is full of teachings about the proper way to regard our resources from the offering system of the Old Testament to the practice of tithing to Jesus' instruction that money and eternal life are connected.

John Wesley also had clear teachings about finances and these are spelled out in his sermon "The Use of Money." Wesley's three rules about money are simple, memorable, and reflect his theology: *gain* all you can, *save* all you can, and *give* all you can. At the heart of these rules is the belief that all of our resources, including money, are gifts of grace from God. When we structure our lives to reflect our faith, including the practice of tithing, we can experience the transformed life the Wesleys talked about. The chapter ends with the Charles Wesley hymn "O For a Thousand Tongues to Sing" which highlights the praise of God who sets our hearts free.

Before Class

- Have Bibles available for group members who may not bring their own.
- Provide markers of varied colors, pencils, pens, and blank paper for use during the session.
- Post the two sheets titled "The Wesleyan Way of Salvation" that you created in previous sessions in a visible place in the room. On the second sheet write the following question and response:

8. What About My Money?

"Money, like grace, is a gift from God. When we structure our lives to reflect our faith, including the practice of tithing, we open ourselves to continuing transformation."

- If you have access to a copier, make a handout of the eight questions and responses included on "The Wesleyan Way of Salvation" sheets. All eight are written out in the Session Themes included in the leader helps at the beginning of this leader's guide on pages 8–9.
- On a large sheet of paper or a section of the whiteboard, write the following title across the top: "Wesley's Three Rules for Being Faithful with Money." Post the sheet in a visible and accessible location in your meeting area.
- On a large sheet of paper or another part of the whiteboard, write the following quotation from Forrest Pool:

"I realized that giving 10% of my income provides me a regular, tangible reminder that my purpose on this planet is not limited by the money I have. It became a commitment between God and me that my reliance on money would never again come between us. I realized that tithing was not a battle over my wallet . . . it was a battle over my heart." —Forrest Pool

- Post the Forrest Pool quotation on the wall.

Welcome

Reflect on Your Most Recent Meal

Invite group members to think about their experience of eating dinner the day before. Ask volunteers to share:

- Where did you eat dinner?
- With whom did you eat?
- What did you have for dinner?
- What did you enjoy about the meal?

Now, ask volunteers to share:

- Approximately how much did you spend on dinner, whether on the bill from a restaurant or the groceries for a meal at home?

Notice the responses of group members to this question. Ask:

- Which of the questions we asked made us most uncomfortable to share about?
- Why do so many of us avoid talking about money or the cost of things?

Say to the group:

- In the eighth chapter of the book, the authors turn to a topic that makes many of us uncomfortable—money. In the opening section of the chapter, they quote Forrest Pool who says:

  "Money . . . During my life, it has been my least favorite thing, my strongest desire, my status symbol, my ticket to the social circle of my choice, my comfort, my stress, my love, and my salvation. It is power and weakness. But more than anything, for me, money has been about control. . . . When anything is all of these things and more to a person, it is extremely personal. Money is personal."

Ask:

- In what ways is Forrest Pool's view of money similar to yours?
- What makes talking about money personal?

Begin with a Prayer

Pray the following prayer or one of your own:

God who created all things and called them "good,"
We confess that we get uncomfortable when we talk about money.

We know the power it has in our lives,

  Whether we feel we have enough or too little.

As we seek the peace and joy of your reign,

  Help us to give this area of our lives to you as well. Amen.

Bible Study and Discussion

Explore the Use of Resources in the Old Testament

Divide into three groups. Say:

- In "The Bible's Teaching" section of chapter 8, the authors look at how the Old Testament talks about the use of resources. In this exercise we're going to look at three different sections of the Old Testament.

Have each group look at one of the following sets of passages:

- Genesis 1:28-31; Genesis 8:20-21
- Proverbs 1:10-19; Ecclesiastes 5:10
- Jeremiah 17:11; Malachi 3:10

Ask them to use the following questions as they explore the passages:

- What do these passages say about the connection between our resources and our hearts?
- What responsibilities do humans have with their resources?
- How does our use of resources impact our relationship with God?

Gather as a large group to share insights from the small group discussions. Ask:

- Based on your exploration of these passages, how would you complete the following sentence: "Since God has given us all things, we should…"?

Consider Jesus and the Rich Young Man

Ask for three volunteers to act out the interaction between Jesus and a young man in Matthew 19:16-22. Give each volunteer one of three roles to read: Narrator, Jesus, and Young Man. Invite group members to turn to the passage in their Bibles and follow along as the volunteers present a dramatic reading of the passage.

Now ask the volunteers to do the reading again, pausing after each statement by Jesus or the Young Man. Ask the group to put the statement they have just heard into their own words. Ask:

- What is the speaker saying here?

After the second reading, thank the volunteers. Now ask:

- What does this story suggest is the connection between money and eternal life?

Video Study and Discussion

Play the video for Session 8.

After viewing the video segment, choose some of the following questions to explore with the group:

- Why is our use of money a good measure of our faith?
- How does our giving help us participate in what God is doing in the world?
- What is the key question to ask when you feel you want to make more money?
- How does the story of the widow's mite help us understand God's attitude toward money?

Book Study and Discussion

Receive a Report on Wesley's Sermon

If a volunteer has read the Wesley sermon "The Use of Money," invite that person to share his or her observations about the sermon. Ask the volunteer to address these questions:

- What was Wesley's central point?
- What were the highlights of the sermon for you?

Examine Wesley's Three Rules for Being Faithful with Money

Say to the group:

- In his sermon "The Use of Money," John Wesley presents three rules for being faithful with money. In the next exercise we will look at these three rules.

Invite participants to turn to the "Wesley's Answer" section of chapter 8 (pages 116–119). Read aloud (or have someone read) the paragraph that begins with the sentence: "Wesley's first rule is, 'gain all you can.' " Write the first rule on the large sheet of paper you posted before the class began with the title "Wesley's Three Rules for Being Faithful with Money." Ask:

- What does Wesley mean by "gain all you can"?
- What does Wesley say about how we should make money?
- What does this rule say about a Christian view of money?

Now read the next paragraph in the book that begins with the sentence: "Wesley's second rule is, 'save all you can' " (page 118). Write the second rule on the large sheet. Ask:

- What does Wesley mean by "save all you can"?
- How is Wesley's understanding different from other understandings of saving money?
- What does this rule say about a Christian view of money?

Next read the following paragraph in the study book, which begins: "Until this point,..." (page 118). Write the third rule—give all you can—on the large sheet. Ask:

- What does Wesley mean by "give all you can"?
- How does this rule relate to the idea of stewardship?
- What does this rule say about a Christian view of money?

Evaluate Your Personal Habits

Distribute blank pieces of paper and writing instruments to participants. Invite them to write down the three rules with space between each one for writing. Ask group members to reflect on how they are living out each area of Wesley's structure in their own lives. Assure the participants that they will not be asked to share what they are writing down.

Ask participants to write down one commitment they could make to grow in each rule. After some time for individual work, come back together as a total group. Invite volunteers to share commitments as they feel comfortable.

Understand the Tithe

Say to the group:

- Tithing is a spiritual practice that has its roots in Scripture. This is the practice in which people give one-tenth of their income or resources to God.

Have group members turn to Nehemiah 10:35-37, either in their Bibles or in "The Bible's Teaching" section of chapter 8 where it is printed (pages 113–114). Invite a volunteer to read it aloud. Ask:

- What do the people commit to bring to God?
- What would it mean for us to give our best to God?

Point out the quotation from Forrest Pool that you posted on the wall before the session started. Ask group members to read it aloud together. Ask:

- How is tithing a battle over your heart?
- What did Forrest Pool come to realize about the meaning of tithing?

Close the Session

Revisit the Lessons of This Class

If you were able to make handouts as suggested in the "Before Class" section of this leader's guide, distribute those to group members now. Otherwise direct the group's attention to the two sheets titled "The Wesleyan Way of Salvation." Read together the answer to question 8, "What About My Money?"

Say to the group:

- The authors of this study began this book with the hope that by returning to John Wesley's methods of taking the Bible seriously we can love God and our neighbors more.

Ask:

- How has this study changed how you read the Bible?
- How has it helped you understand what the Bible means by salvation?

Close with a Prayer

Invite each class member to consider one thing that he or she would like to keep from the experience of this study. Invite group members to close their eyes and offer this one thing aloud in the form of a prayer to God. Model the prayer yourself by beginning in the form, "Lord, I give you thanks for this group and this study. I want to keep..."

After everyone has had a chance to share, close the prayer in the following way:

Lord, we want to love you and our neighbors more. Bless us in your way. Amen.

Read a Hymn

As a group, read or sing together Charles Wesley's hymn, "O For a Thousand Tongues to Sing" as it is printed at the conclusion of chapter 8.

Sermons of John Wesley

Below is a list of the fifty-three sermons published by John Wesley in 1771, which contain the forty-four commonly regarded as the "Standard Sermons" as well as an additional nine that Wesley added at that time. The order they appear reflects the order in which they appeared in the 1771 edition, which is preserved in the first four volumes of *The Bicentennial Edition of the Works of John Wesley* (Nashville: Abingdon, 1984-1987).

1. Salvation by Faith (Ephesians 2:8)
2. The Almost Christian (Acts 26:28)
3. "Awake, Thou That Sleepest" (Ephesians 5:14)
4. Scriptural Christianity (Acts 4:31)
5. Justification by Faith (Romans 4:5)
6. The Righteousness of Faith (Romans 10:5-8)
7. The Way to the Kingdom (Mark 1:15)
8. The First-fruits of the Spirit (Romans 8:1)
9. The Spirit of Bondage and of Adoption (Romans 8:15)
10. The Witness of the Spirit, Discourse I (Romans 8:16)
11. The Witness of the Spirit, Discourse II (Romans 8:16)
12. The Witness of Our Own Spirit (2 Corinthians 1:12)
13. On Sin in Believers (2 Corinthians 5:17)
14. The Repentance of Believers (Mark 1:15)
15. The Great Assize (Romans 14:10)
16. The Means of Grace (Malachi 3:7)
17. The Circumcision of the Heart (Romans 2:29)

18. The Marks of The New Birth (John 3:8)

19. The Great Privilege of Those That Are Born of God (1 John 3:9)

21. Upon Our Lord's Sermon on The Mount, I (Matthew 5:1-4)

22. Upon Our Lord's Sermon on The Mount, II (Matthew 5:5-7)

23. Upon Our Lord's Sermon on The Mount, III (Matthew 5:8-12)

24. Upon Our Lord's Sermon on The Mount, IV (Matthew 5:13-16)

25. Upon Our Lord's Sermon on The Mount, V (Matthew 5:17-20)

26. Upon Our Lord's Sermon on The Mount, VI (Matthew 6:1-15)

27. Upon Our Lord's Sermon on The Mount, VII (Matthew 6:16-18)

28. Upon Our Lord's Sermon on The Mount, VIII (Matthew 6:19-23)

29. Upon Our Lord's Sermon on The Mount, IX (Matthew 6:24-34)

30. Upon Our Lord's Sermon on The Mount, X (Matthew 7:1-12)

31. Upon Our Lord's Sermon on The Mount, XI (Matthew 7:13-14)

32. Upon Our Lord's Sermon on The Mount, XII (Matthew 7:15-20)

33. Upon Our Lord's Sermon on The Mount, XIII (Matthew 7:21-27)

34. The Original, Nature, Property, and Use of the Law (Romans 7:12)

35. The Law Established Through Faith, Discourse I (Romans 3:31)

36. The Law Established Through Faith, Discourse II (Romans 3:31)

37. The Nature of Enthusiasm (Acts 26:24)

38. A Caution Against Bigotry (Mark 9:38-39)

39. Catholic Spirit (2 Kings 10:15)

40. Christian Perfection (Philippians 3:12)

41. Wandering Thoughts (2 Corinthians 10:5)

42. Satan's Devices (2 Corinthians 2:11)

44. Original Sin (Genesis 6:5)

45. The New Birth (John 3:7)

46. The Wilderness State (John 16:22)

47. Heaviness Through Manifold Temptations (1 Peter 1:6)

48. Self-denial (Luke 9:23)

49. The Cure of Evil-speaking (Matthew 18:15-17)

50. The Use of Money (Luke 16:9)

51. The Good Steward (Luke 16:2)

52. The Reformation of Manners (Psalm 94:16)

53. On the Death of George Whitefield (Numbers 23:10)